THE HEYDAY OF THE
BRITISH LORRY:
HISTORIC COMMERCIAL VEHICLES IN COLOUR

Peter Durham and Malcolm Broad

IAN ALLAN
Publishing

Below:
This 1935 Austin Seven 5cwt van is owned by R. F. Edge & Co of Bolton, Lancashire. First owned by the Odeon cinema in Bolton and used for the distribution of film posters nothing more is known of its history until restoration by the present owners. Based on the Austin Seven car, which was introduced in 1922, the first van of 1923 was of 2½cwt capacity and was powered by a 696cc four-cylinder engine rated at 7.2hp. The capacity of the van was upgraded to 5cwt in 1930 with Austin Seven production of all types peaking in 1935. Approximately 291,000 were made in total, the last being built on 3 March 1939.
All photographs by Peter Durham

Previous page:
This 1947 Dennis Max 7½-ton brewer's dray is now owned by Mr D. Cox of Shaftesbury, Dorset. New to Ushers Brewery at Trowbridge, Wiltshire, the vehicle has been restored to its original condition.

The Dennis Max was first introduced in October 1934 and was gradually improved over the next few years, receiving the O4 6.502 litre four-cylinder diesel engine as standard from November 1936. Supplied to the armed forces during World War 2 as a 6-ton 4x2 truck, the Max was upgraded again in late 1945 with a new cab as seen here. A six-cylinder diesel, the 7.585 litre Dennis O6, was available in the Max 6 from 1949 and the range continued in production until 1955 with some examples of the Max 6 being built to special order up until 1958.

First published 1996

ISBN 0 7110 2 386 7

© Peter Durham and Malcolm Broad 1996

Designed by Alan C. Butcher

Published by Ian Allan Publishing

an imprint of Ian Allan Ltd, Terminal House, Station Approach, Shepperton, Surrey TW17 8AS. Printed by Ian Allan Printing Ltd, Coombelands House, Coombelands Lane, Addlestone, Surrey KT15 1HY.

Representing one of the most successful motor vehicles ever built and a pioneer in the field of mass production techniques, this 1915 Ford Model T van is owned by Mr P. Neville of Walton-on-Thames, Surrey, and was photographed on Madeira Drive, Brighton, having just completed the Historic Commercial Vehicle Society's 1993 London to Brighton Run. Found and restored in the late 1980s by the present owner with a typical delivery van body from 1915, it was originally built by the Ford Motor Co at Trafford Park, Manchester, where production of the right-hand drive version commenced in 1911.

The Model T was first introduced in the USA in 1908 and production continued until 1927, by which time over 15 million had been built.

Introduction

The purpose of this book is to portray the preserved historic commercial vehicle in settings which attempt to recreate images of the days when they were still at work. The wonderful colour photographs of working vehicles taken in the 1960s by Peter J. Davies really capture the feel of the vehicles, their surroundings and the period depicted and whilst many of the old dockside and industrial locations have either been altered or have disappeared altogether, it is still possible to photograph historic vehicles in suitable surroundings. However, to recreate the look of a working vehicle is a little more difficult, as they were often a little grimy and the ropes and sheets used to secure their loads were usually in pale colours, unlike the brightly coloured plastic-coated sheets and polypropylene ropes of today.

A relatively inexpensive colour slide film was not really available until the early 1960s, which means that colour archive material concentrates almost entirely on postwar vehicles. Today we have the advantage of being able to select historic commercial vehicles from even the very beginnings of mechanised transport but, having noted that, examples of solid-tyred vehicles dated from, say, prior to 1925 are now less often seen out and about.

Nevertheless, the UK is by far the most important location for historic commercial vehicles in Europe, so there is a vast fleet from which to choose, with new restorations coming on to the preservation scene all the time.

The many summer rallies featuring historic commercial vehicles are testimony to this great interest and in recognition of this a few of the photographs included in this book were taken at rallies. Rallies represent the most obvious way for the public and other enthusiasts to see the vehicles at first hand. Our grateful thanks are extended to all the vehicle owners and rally organisers whose wonderful co-operation has made this book possible.

The preservation of our historic commercial vehicle heritage really began in the late 1950s with the first organised event taking place at the Leyland Motors factory in Lancashire. The first national body for enthusiasts was the Historic Commercial Vehicle Club, established in 1958, and its present day Society equivalent consists of over 4,000 members. It was in the Society's journal, *Historic Commercial News*, that the idea of specifically created photographs of the type featured in this book was first put into practice at the beginning of 1994 under the title *'Historic Commercials on Location'*, and the enthusiasm with which this series was greeted provided the impetus for the book.

Our selection concentrates on commercial vehicles in all their road-going forms, with the exception of buses since these warrant a book in their own right. The vehicle types are grouped together in the following order: vans and light commercials, including ambulances and taxis; lorries and vans under 3 tons carrying capacity; lorries and vans over 3 tons carrying capacity in two-, three- and four-axle form, plus articulated vehicles; special purpose vehicles; fire engines; and, last but not least, military vehicles. We have tried to select as broad a band as possible of vehicle makes and types, bearing in mind that the generally recognised minimum age requirement for vehicles to be considered 'historic' is 20 years. However, as this is a rolling date there are many vehicles in existence and being restored that are not quite yet of the necessary age, but are none the less significant in the development of the commercial vehicle and if future volumes are possible, these will take their turn.

One aspect of the commercial vehicle industry in the UK that is often overlooked when one sees the number of overseas vehicles on our roads today, is that this is nothing new. In the early days of mechanised road transport French and German makes like Berliet and Daimler-Benz were prominent, then, in the interwar period, a number of North American makes like Diamond T and Reo were imported and, in some cases, assembled here. The famous Bedford was a British-built General Motors product developed from the corporation's Chevrolet truck and it was only really in the period from 1945 until 1965 that the UK market was almost wholly home produced.

It is from this period that the majority of preserved commercial vehicles are seen today. Particularly pleasing are the number of heavy commercials now being preserved, often due to the efforts of transport-related companies who have the financial resources and facilities to achieve this. However, the amateur restorer must be given full recognition and there are many examples of 'back garden' restoration in our selection.

Photographs in this book have been taken using medium format cameras: a Bronica ETRSi and Mamiya 645 PRO, with Fuji and Agfa film, of varying ASA settings, according to the available light and weather conditions.

However, one 35mm transparency has been selected, this using a Nikon F4S with 50mm 1.4 lens and Fuji film. Such is the quality of 35mm transparency film today, it may therefore be difficult to identify in this collection.

It has always been my objective to place these superb restored vehicles away from a rally field and, into suitable period settings, free from modern street furniture and the ubiquitous 'yellow line'. This is not as easy as it may sound so I would like to thank the many owners whose patience I have extended to the limit whilst out on photographic road runs. Without such assistance, so readily given, this collection of photographs would not have been possible.

Malcolm Broad
Peter Durham
August 1995

This 1936 Morris-Commercial T2 1-ton dropside lorry is owned by Mr G. Smith of Lambourn, Berkshire. Photographed during a quiet moment on the 1993 HCVS Ridgeway Run from Oxford to Newbury, this vehicle was first owned by a coal merchant in Salisbury and was later sold to a farmer. It was then left to disintegrate until 1969 when purchased by the present owner and restored over a 12-year period. The T2 was an improved version of the original Morris-Commercial T Type Tonner first introduced in 1924 and was in production from 1931 until 1938. Being a late example of this model, note that this one is equipped with four-wheel brakes.

Owned by Messrs R. and E. Rawlins of Pangbourne, Berkshire, this 1937 Bedford BYC 12cwt market gardener's truck has been restored to the original livery it carried when in the ownership of B. Burrows of Stratford-upon-Avon, by whom it was used for sheep and market produce transport. We thought that we should entitle this photograph 'Not on' — can you see why?

The Bedford BYC was available from 1934 until 1939 and was powered by the 2.4 litre Big Six Vauxhall engine, the outwardly similar BXC being Bedford powered.

This 1938 Morris Minor 5cwt GPO linesman's van is owned by Mr S. Smallwood of Micklefield, near Leeds. Specially produced for the Post Office and known as External Utilities, they were supplied between August 1934 and February 1940 and carried special 35cu ft bodies by various bodybuilders, including Harold Perry, Duple, Bonallack and Park Royal. An interesting feature was the angled top to the windscreen, which enabled overhead wires to be inspected from within the vehicle. This example features the Easiclean wheels fitted from about December 1937, which replaced the earlier wire variety. The van was found in Bangor in 1971, restored and has been with the present owner since 1991.

This 1939 1-ton battery electric van was built, and is still owned by, Harrods of Knightsbridge.

The famous Harrods department store began using battery-electric vehicles in the 1920s. These first vehicles were Walker model K vans built in the USA. When it was decided to replace these in the late 1930s, Harrods' own staff designed and built 60 new vans between 1936 and 1941. These vans were powered by a 3½hp electric motor and had a range of 60 miles at a level speed of 18.6mph with a full 1-ton payload. They were a familiar sight in the capital for many years and at least three examples have survived into preservation.

This is a 1952 Morris-Commercial PV 15/20cwt van owned by Mr and Mrs P. Neale of North Weald, Essex. The PV (or 'Parcel Van') was first introduced in 1939 but, due to the war, was not actually listed until 1946, continuing in production until August 1953. It was designed to compete with battery-electric vehicles in the retail door-to-door trade and had a functional 235cu ft body, with sliding doors for easy access. This gave it a somewhat utilitarian look in keeping with postwar austerity.

This example was new to Wittens bakers in Skegness and was used by them until 1961. It was rescued for preservation in 1988 and was given to the present owners in pieces in 1991 as a silver wedding present!

Owned and restored by Messrs J. and I. Cox and M. Turner of Alderholt, Hampshire, this is a 1952 Jowett Bradford CC type 5cwt van. Produced from 1946 until 1953 by Jowett Cars Ltd of Idle, near Bradford — a firm better known for its Javelin cars — these little vans were powered by a two-cylinder horizontally-opposed 1,005cc petrol engine and were also available with dropside or utility bodywork.

Photographed at the ford at Moyles Court in the New Forest, this van was new to a firm of amusement caterers in Bournemouth but spent most of its working life with a market gardener in Alderholt until 1963. It was purchased for preservation in 1972 with only 48,000 miles on the clock.

Right:
This 1954 Austin A40 10cwt van is owned and was restored by Mr R. Webb of Maidenhead, Berkshire. The A40 van was introduced in March 1948 with a pick-up version following six months later. Both were based on the A40 car and had frontal styling similar to the Devon variant. A column gearchange was introduced in 1951, but whereas the Austin Devon car ceased production in 1952, the commercial version continued up to March 1957.

Until 1988 this example had had one owner from new, who had fitted windows to the nearside panels and added extra seats to convert it into an estate car. It was then acquired for preservation and restored to van condition. It was photographed during the HCVS South Midlands Area Ridgeway Run from Oxford to Newbury in June 1993.

Left:
When photographed, this 1955 Ford Thames E83W 10cwt van was owned by John Lord of Leicester. Restored in 1994, it visited just one rally before being sold to a new owner in Ireland. It was new to the Home Office, being one of six supplied by Ford as part of contract No 25689.

Announced in March 1938, the E83W continued in production almost unchanged until September 1957 — a run of over 19 years. It was of semi-forward control design with the 10hp 1,172cc four-cylinder side-valve engine offset to allow the driver's pedals to be alongside the engine. The grille featured two starting handle slots to cater for left- and right-hand drive versions. The E83W was available in several forms, including van, chassis cab (mainly for dropside bodywork), pick-up and personnel carrier; examples of all of these have survived into preservation.

Fitted with an all-metal body produced exclusively by Auto Services of Westbourne, Bournemouth, this 1956 Morris-Commercial J-type 10cwt open dairy vehicle spent its working life with Coward Bros dairy of Shaftesbury. It then spent many years in a Wiltshire scrapyard. In 1991 it was purchased by Mr G. Swale of Trowbridge, who has restored it to original condition, including the heavy duty tyres specified by Cowards to provide extra traction in wet and wintry conditions on the many steep hills encountered on the rounds.

The Morris-Commercial J-type was introduced in October 1949 and was powered by a 1,476cc four-cylinder side-valve engine. Production continued until 1957 when it was superseded by the outwardly similar JB — which was fitted with an overhead-valve engine — that was available until 1961. A version was also produced by Austin. In van form these vehicles became an everyday sight in service, particularly with the Post Office and today have a very strong following among enthusiasts. There is even a 'J–type Register'.

Left:
This 1961 Ford Thames 402E 15cwt, with factory-fitted dropside bodywork, is owned by Mr M. Doel of Bradford-on-Avon. The first owner of the vehicle was a market gardener of Botley Road, Southampton, who operated it for 21 years, mainly during the summer months. During this time it covered just 21,000 miles. The next three owners also came from Botley Road, so the Thames spent a total of 29 years in the same street until it was sold to a number plate dealer in Dorset in 1990. By the time the present owner purchased it in 1992 it had lost its original registration number, 6483 TR. It has since been restored with all the original owners providing information on its history, including the original bill of sale dated 7 July 1961. It has still only covered 29,000 miles.

The 400E range was introduced in 1957 and was powered by the Ford Consul engine. It came in two models — the 10/12cwt and the 15cwt — and quickly became a popular successor to the old E83W range. A Perkins diesel option was offered in 1961 and the vehicle was available in a host of different bodywork configurations. A more powerful Zephyr 4 engine was available from January 1963 and the 400E range continued in production until August 1965 when it was replaced by the Ford Transit.

Right:
Owned by Mr R. Bolton of Retford, this Triumph Courier 5cwt van was first registered in 1962 to a Nottingham owner who used it in connection with his business as an electrical contractor. Transferred to a private user in 1964, it was sold again in the 1980s to a Triumph enthusiast who used it as his personal transport until it was purchased by the present owner in 1992. For two years the Courier was used daily as a parts/service vehicle in the business of a classic vehicle dealer and restoration specialist, but as the business is now only run part time the vehicle is now in semi-retirement and used only for pleasure purposes and rallies.

This van was originally supplied by the local Retford dealer and by chance has ended up back in its own area. The Triumph Courier was based on the well-known Herald car and was powered by a four-cylinder 1,147cc engine. However, only approximately 4,600 Couriers were produced between 1962 and mid-1967, and even then the last 1,000 were returned to the factory and converted into estate cars as they could not be sold as vans. The Triumph Sports Six Club records show that only 12 vans are known to be running at the present time.

Below:

Dating from 1969, this Morris 1000 6cwt van was one of a type known to the Post Office as the '50 cubic foot'. This example spent its working life around Warwick and Leamington Spa, before being withdrawn in 1976. Eight owners followed, including a builder and farmer, but it has now been restored by its present owner, Mr P. Wood of Mitcham, Surrey, who is seen here in suitable period uniform, complete with letters and keys, alongside the van.

Introduced in May 1953 and based upon the Morris Minor car, the van was originally rated at 5cwt and fitted with an 800cc four-cylinder overhead-valve engine. The engine capacity was increased to 948cc in 1958 when it became known as the Morris Minor 1000. Later models had a 1,098cc engine and the van payload was increased to 6cwt in 1962, with an 8cwt version with heavier duty springs and tyres also becoming available. The Austin-badged version, with a slightly different grille, was introduced in 1968 and production of both the van and pick-up versions continued until 1971.

The Royal Mail Morris Minor/1000 van became one of the best known commercial vehicles in Great Britain and was the standard small van for almost 20 years, with nearly 28,000 also being supplied to Post Office Telephones.

Right:

This 1935 Talbot AY95 ambulance is owned by the London Ambulance Service. New to the London County Council, it served right through the war years, eventually being retired in 1949. It then became part of the London Ambulance Vintage Fleet and has appeared in several films depicting the war years. Only two of this model are known to exist, the other example being a military ambulance at the Army Transport Museum at Beverley, Humberside.

Produced by Clement-Talbot Ltd of North Kensington, London, from 1934 until 1937, the AY95 ambulance featured a low-height chassis, 20.9hp six-cylinder engine and a four-speed synchromesh gearbox with a preselect gearbox available for an additional £25.00.

Fitted with bodywork by Appleyard of Leeds, this 1954 Morris LD1 Ambulance is owned by Mr P. Honey of Slough. New to the City of Bristol, it was one of a batch of eight and served until 1972. It was then sold to a company which specialised in renting out vehicles to the film industry, but ended up in a High Wycombe scrapyard until purchased in 1989 by its present owner. It was fully restored over a two-year period.

Introduced in July 1953, the Morris LD1 was a 1-ton capacity model powered by a 2.199 litre four-cylinder petrol engine. The model continued in production until January 1955 when it was replaced by an updated version with revised frontal styling that was also marketed by Austin and available with a BMC 2.178 litre diesel option. The LD range then continued to be available until the summer of 1968, but examples of the earlier LD1 version, as illustrated here, are now very rare.

Dating from 1935 and owned since 1991 by Mr P. McWilliam of Pontefract, West Yorkshire, this Austin 12/4 LL Landaulet taxi, fitted with a Vincent body, served in London until approximately 1956. It was sold to its previous owner in 1959 and underwent a full restoration in the mid-1960s.

The first purpose-built Austin taxi was based on the 12/4 car chassis and introduced in 1929. However, the type's turning circle had to be reduced before Scotland Yard would grant it a licence to operate in London, but once this was resolved Austins became the most popular make of taxi in the metropolis.

In 1934 the introduction of a worm drive rear axle enabled a low body to be fitted, providing a flat floor in the passenger compartment. This type was in production until 1938, becoming known as the 'LL' or 'Low-Loader', with many examples serving the Capital through the 1950s and into the 1960s.

Dating from 1927, this Thornycroft A1/FB4 30cwt van is owned by Mr T. Mansbridge of Basingstoke, Hampshire. The production records for the vehicle state that it was delivered new to Vick Brothers, probably the haulage company of that name, trading in Aldershot at the time. It has been restored in the livery of the Great Western Railway, one of Thornycroft's largest customers, which used the A1 model on Express Cartage Services. For these operations bodies were constructed at Swindon Works. Earlier examples had solid tyres, open driving compartments, oil-lamp lighting and were limited to 12mph. However, later refinements included windscreens and side doors to the cab, electric lighting and pneumatic tyres, uprating the vehicle's speed to 20mph.

The type was introduced in 1924 with a 22.5hp four-cylinder engine and continued in production until 1931. John I. Thornycroft Ltd, of Basingstoke, was one of the country's leading commercial vehicle manufacturers and also one of the oldest, being founded in 1864 as the Steam Carriage & Waggon Co at Church Wharf, Chiswick.

Delivered new to a haulier from Chelsea and reputedly used for deliveries from West End stores like Harrods, this 1928 Dennis C 30cwt dropside lorry is owned by Mr J. Trethewy of St Austell, Cornwall, who restored it to its present condition.

Dennis Bros Ltd of Guildford, Surrey, began producing commercial vehicles in 1904 and by the late 1920s had become the country's leading manufacturer, with an output of over 100 chassis per week in 1928. The 30cwt was particularly successful; it was powered by a four-cylinder 17.9hp engine and equipped with a worm drive rear axle. This was a feature of Dennis vehicles right from the earliest days of production, the company never using the more primitive chain drive used by most of the competition.

Introduced in 1925, the 30cwt continued in production until 1933, a forward control version being introduced in 1930.

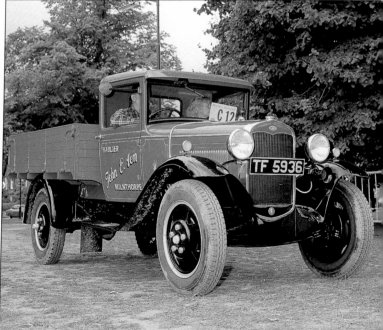

Below:
Owned by Mr J. E. Ion of Milnthorpe, Cumbria, this 1931 Ford AA 30cwt dropside lorry was photographed at The Stray in Harrogate after completing the HCVS Trans-Pennine Run in August 1993. New to Shepherds (Fruiterers) of Fleetwood in Lancashire, it was later owned by Whiteside Bros of Stalmine, Fleetwood, and used for general farm duties. It has been fully restored by its current owner.

Introduced in late 1927, the Ford AA, with four-cylinder 24hp engine, was initially produced at Trafford Park, Manchester, until in October 1931 production was transferred to the Ford Motor Co's new plant at Dagenham, Essex. Early examples had wire-spoked wheels and a three-speed transmission, with disc wheels and a four-speed transmission being introduced in 1929. Production continued until 1935.

Left:
This 1946 Commer Q2 2-ton dropside lorry was restored and is owned by Mr M. Tilly of Corsham, Wiltshire. Unfortunately nothing is known of the vehicle's working history other than at one stage it worked on a farm.

Commer, based at Luton in Bedfordshire, was another old-established commercial vehicle manufacturer and was founded in 1905 under the name Commercial Cars Ltd. It was acquired by Humber in 1926, becoming part of the Rootes Group in 1928. The Q model (also known as the Superpoise) was introduced in April 1939 and provided a stylish range of vehicles from 30cwt to 6-ton capacity. They were widely used by the armed forces during World War 2, particularly the Q4 3-tonner.

The Q2 was powered by a 20.92hp six-cylinder engine, uprated to 27hp in 1942 and it continued in production until 1948.

Below:
Photographed at Portsmouth Harbour, home for this 1936 Bedford WLG 2-ton dropside lorry is the Amberley Chalk Pits Museum, near Arundel, Sussex. New to W. H. & J. Goodwin, corn merchants of Ash, near Sevenoaks, Kent, it continued in service with them right up to 1969 when the company ceased trading. The vehicle was then sold for scrap but was rescued by Bernard J. Newman, builder's merchants of Horsham, and has been further restored by the Museum. The WLG, along with the shorter wheelbase WHG, was the first model produced by Bedford in 1931 and was fitted with its six-cylinder overhead-valve 26.3hp engine. The type was an instant success, replacing vehicles that owed their origins to the solid-tyred, chain-driven era. The model continued in production until 1939, undergoing many improvements along the way and by the end of the decade the Bedford slogan 'You see them everywhere' was most certainly appropriate.

Owned by Mr D. Stone of Glastonbury, Somerset, this 1948 Bedford MSD 2-ton dropside lorry was exported to Jersey, where it carried the registration number J10109 and used by G. Le Marquand, potato growers of St Martins, to transport potatoes from the farm to the ferry. It has been restored to that livery by its present owner.

The Bedford M type was introduced in late 1939 in two wheelbase forms — 10ft and 11ft 11in — powered by the six-cylinder 28hp overhead-valve engine. Production was suspended from 1940 until 1945 to enable Bedford to concentrate on military types but resumed in 1945 and continued until 1952. The pre-1940 model, which is rare, can be identified by the lack of horizontal chrome bars on the radiator grille.

This 1968 Karrier Bantam fuel tanker is owned by Mr N. Miles, of Rangeworthy, Gloucestershire. Operated from new by Yeo Fuels, Moretonhampstead, Devon, this vehicle was used on domestic fuel oil deliveries right up until 1 January 1993, when it was eventually replaced by an IVECO Daily.

Karrier Motors Ltd started life in 1908 as Clayton & Co (Huddersfield) Ltd and moved to Luton in 1934 after being acquired by the Rootes Group. Under Rootes' ownership the Karrier name became particularly associated with municipal and urban delivery vehicles and the Bantam range, introduced in 1936, quickly became

established in this field. The range was updated in 1948 and equipped with an all-steel cab similar to that fitted to contemporary forward-control Commer lorries, also part of the Rootes Group. The range was further updated in 1958 and fitted with the design of cab seen in the vehicle illustrated.

In this form the Bantam was powered by either a 2.266 litre four-cylinder petrol engine or a 2.260 litre diesel. A lightweight tractor unit was used by British Rail in a 'mechanical horse' role. Production of the Bantam finally came to an end in April 1978.

Owned by Thomas Wethered & Son Ltd, Marlow, Buckinghamshire, this 1919 Thornycroft J type 4-ton brewery dray, was purchased new by the company and was in daily use until 1946, when it was returned to Thornycroft at Basingstoke and housed in the company's museum. The same driver — Mr J. Lennard — both collected and returned the vehicle, duties spanning 27 years! About 25 years ago it was returned to the brewer and restored. During its working life the original solid tyres were replaced by pneumatics, and electric lighting, a speedometer and cab glazing were added.

The J type was developed in 1912 and an example successfully competed in the War Office trials of that year and, when sold to Pickfords in 1913, became the first subsidy vehicle. This scheme allowed purchases of chassis built to an approved design to receive a certain sum of money on condition that the government could purchase the vehicle in the event of a national emergency. Subsidy vehicles, built by many different manufacturers, were used in their thousands during World War 1, and upon disposal after hostilities ceased provided the fledgling road haulage industry in this country with large numbers of proven and reliable vehicles.

Originally powered by a 32.4hp four-cylinder side-valve engine, the J type received an updated 36.1hp power unit in 1921 and continued in production until 1927.

Delivered new to W. J. King of Bishop's Lydeard, Somerset, this 1925 Foden C-type 6-ton three-way tipper is now owned by Mr J. Wait of Bristol. W. J. King owned quarries and, at its peak, operated 30 steam waggons of six different makes. In 1931 the business ceased using steam waggons except for a few Sentinels that were fitted with pneumatic tyres and continued in use up to World War 2. After they ceased working, the steamers did not move again until they were auctioned in May 1988 in one of the most interesting historic vehicle sales for many years. MB 9404, maker's No 11850, has since been completely restored to its original livery.

Fodens Ltd, of Elworth Works, Sandbach, Cheshire, produced its first steam waggons in 1901 and later became the largest manufacturer of steam vehicles in the world. Introduced in 1920, the C-type was one of its most successful designs, continuing in production until Foden ceased steam waggon manufacture in 1933.

This 1931 Sentinel DG4P 6-7-ton flat-platform steam waggon is owned by D. & D. Goddard & Son of Shrewsbury, Shropshire. Works No 8571, this waggon was new to Samuel Banner Ltd in Liverpool and subsequently passed to Paull Bros Ltd, Homepride Flour Mills, Birkenhead. Like many of its contemporaries in the Liverpool area, this waggon had a long working life and was purchased for preservation in 1949. It was owned by the well-known steam waggon preservationist, the late Mr E. N. Shone, and restored in Paull Bros's livery. In 1977 it passed to the present owners and was restored in the colours of Morris of Shrewsbury, a firm which also used Sentinel waggons.

The first Sentinels were produced in 1906 by Alley & McClellan Ltd at Polmadie, Glasgow, but production was transferred in 1915 to the Sentinel Waggon Works in Shrewsbury, where production had reached 32 per week by 1920. The DG (double-geared) model was introduced in 1927 in both four- and six-wheeled form and in 1929 came the DG8, acknowledged as the first rigid eight-wheeler, with production of the DG continuing until the early 1930s.

Now owned by the Lincolnshire Road Transport Museum, this 1934 AEC Monarch 7½-ton tipper was owned and operated for most of its working life by Bracebridge Mental Hospital, Lincoln, and used for the collection of coke from the gas works to fire the boilers. Powered by a 5.1 litre four-cylinder petrol engine, this is an example of the model 647 Monarch, of which 166 were built between 1933 and 1935.

The Monarch range was first introduced in 1931 and was designed by the brilliant engineer, John Rackham. It continued to be available until the war stopped civilian goods chassis production in 1942. The range was reintroduced in 1945, with the final version, the Mark III powered by the famous AEC 7.7 litre diesel engine, being available from 1947 until 1956.

Owned by Mr V. Gould of Camerton, Somerset, this 1934 Sentinel S4 7-ton steam waggon has been restored to the livery of the original owners, the Cowlairs Co-operative Society in Glasgow, which used it for coal and coke deliveries.

Introduced in 1933, the Sentinel S-type represented the pinnacle of British steam waggon design and featured a fully-enclosed cab with the vertical boiler situated behind the driver and an underfloor mounted four-cylinder poppet-valve engine. Transmission was by shaft drive and pneumatic tyres were fitted as standard. A total of 400 S-types were built in four-, six- and eight-wheeled versions until 1938, but in 1950 a further batch of 100 was built for export to Argentina.

Delivered new to Highgate Ales of Walsall, this 1934 Albion LHB463 3-ton brewery dray is now owned by Mr S. Constable of Kingswood Common, near Wolverhampton. It was used by the brewery until 1950 when it passed to a farmer in Halesowen and rapidly deteriorated. A Cleobury Mortimer haulier then bought it and sold it to a Dawley scrap dealer. Its present owner then purchased it for preservation and restoration took 12 months. Mitchell & Butlers, now owners of Highgate Ales, asked if it could be repainted in the original blue livery and it has since been used for promotional work on behalf of M&B and has appeared on television. The lorry carries an authentic brewery load of five hogsheads, seven barrels and five firkins.

Introduced in 1932, the LHB463 had an Albion four-cylinder petrol engine of 22.5hp and a wheelbase of 14ft. A four-cylinder diesel option (referred to by Albion at the time as an oil engine) was made available in 1934 and the type remained in production until 1935.

This 1936 Leyland Beaver TSC9 7-ton tanker is now owned by Dixon Fuel Oils of Northampton. Originally a flat platform lorry, it then served with the same family of showmen from 1940 until 1976 when it was purchased by the present owners. It has been restored to represent the type of tanker operated by Dixons until the mid-1950s, with the tank dating from about 1945. For many years this lorry was powered by a non-standard Gardner 5LW diesel engine, but in May 1995 this was replaced by a Leyland 8.6 litre diesel, one of three power units available for the Beaver during the production run from 1933 to 1939.

A vehicle that would have had a Gardner 5LW engine as standard is this 1936 ERF CI5 7-ton three-way tipper owned by C. G. Holton & Sons Ltd of Milton Keynes. New to W. J. King of Bishop's Lydeard, Somerset, it was used on council contracts and was later sold to K. T. Cook & Son of Eversley near Basingstoke with whom it worked until the late 1970s, also being rallied as a working vehicle. It was then parked in a field for 13 years until being restored by the present owners in conjunction with ERF Ltd. With chassis number 511, this lorry is quite an early example of the ERF philosophy of building a vehicle around the best proprietary components, in this case Gardner engine, David Brown gearbox and a Kirkstall overhead worm rear axle. The CI5 was introduced in 1933 and continued in production until 1947, ERF being one of the few commercial vehicle manufacturers allowed to supply the civilian market during World War 2.

Owned by Mr J. Thomas of Guyhirn, near Wisbech, Cambridgeshire, this 1936 Vulcan 3RF 3-ton flat was new to Soames & Co Ltd, table water bottlers of Wisbech, and used as a delivery dray. It has been restored to its original livery by the present owner, who acquired it derelict from a London scrapyard. Only two of this model are known to survive and both were originally Soames vehicles. Powered by Vulcan's own design of 3.4 litre four-cylinder side-valve petrol engine, this would have been one of the last vehicles produced at the company's Crossens, Southport, factory before the company went into receivership. The production rights were then bought by Tilling-Stevens and the Vulcan operation was transferred to Victoria Works, Maidstone, where production continued until 1953 (see also page 44).

Now restored by its current owner, Mr R. Horton of Brierley Hill, West Midlands, this 1936 Diamond T model 56 3-ton dropside lorry was supplied new to its first owner by Herefordshire agents, Praills. After six months it passed following HP snatchback to R. W. Salisbury of Staunton Court, Gloucester and was used on general haulage until 1962 when it was purchased by the present owner in a derelict condition from behind a garage in Leominster, Herefordshire. It has now been rallied for some 20 years.

Production of Diamond T trucks commenced in 1911 in Chicago and the model 56 was introduced in 1936, being one of the models available in the UK, along with similar types from other US manufacturers like Pierce-Arrow and Reo. Powered by a 27hp six-cylinder Hercules petrol engine, the model 56 remained in production until 1938. Diamond T later became well known during World War 2 for its military trucks, particularly tank transporter tractors and recovery vehicles, a number of which have also survived into preservation.

This 1939 Albion FT3 6-ton flat lorry is now owned by Mr T. R. Reading, of Aylesbury, Buckinghamshire. New to haulier Arthur Pershore of Bilston, the subsequent owners were Ex-Army Transport, North Western Transport Services, Taylor-Walker and Ind-Coope brewery (Burton-on-Trent), finally being used as a coal lorry in the Derby area. It was bought by the present owner in a derelict state and restored over an 18-month period, being put back on the road in 1991.

The Alison FT3 was introduced in 1939 and was powered by the Albion EN277 six-cylinder side-valve petrol engine of 4.25 litre capacity with a 29.4hp rating.

The model was produced in limited numbers during World War 2 and continued to be available from 1945 until about 1952.

Owned by Mr R. Lea, of Newport, Shropshire, this 1946 Dodge 101 5-ton flat platform lorry was new to Shorthall Bros, of Stone, Staffordshire, who were corn merchants. It remained with them until 1956 collecting animal feeds from Liverpool, during which period it covered over 300,000 miles. It then passed to Ernest Knight, a farmer from Bromere Heath in Shropshire, where, after its working life, it was allowed to rot away until restored by its present owner in 1990.

The Dodge 101 was introduced in 1940 and was available with a Perkins P6 4.73 litre six-cylinder diesel engine or a Chrysler 3.89 litre side-valve six-cylinder petrol engine, as in the vehicle illustrated. The 100/101 models were used by the armed forces during World War 2, together with the 6-ton 120/121 and the 3-ton 80/82 types and remained in production at the Dodge plant at Mortlake Road, Kew, until 1951.

New to A. Evans & Son, of Bishops Castle, Shropshire, this 1947 Foden DG4/7½ flat spent all its working life with them as a box van collecting eggs and game from Welsh border farmers on Mondays and Tuesdays then delivering the produce all round the Midlands on Wednesdays, Thursdays and Fridays. It was retired in 1968 and then stored before restoration commenced in 1993, being completed on 4 August 1994 when this photograph was taken at Ditton Priors, Shropshire.

The Foden DG was introduced in 1937 and firmly established Fodens as a builder of quality diesel-engined commercial vehicles. The earlier R and S type models, built after the prototype diesel lorry of 1931, were heavy and expensive to produce and the company nearly did not survive the transition from a steam waggon builder to manufacturer of diesel lorries. However, the DG range was a great success and was available in four-, six- and eight-wheeled form with Gardner three-, four-, five- and six-cylinder LW engines as options. It remained in production until 1947 with large numbers of militarised DG4/6 6-tonners and DG6/12 10-ton six-wheelers being supplied to the armed forces during World War 2.

Owned by Mr D. Roberts-Malpass, of Kingswinford, West Midlands, this 1949 Thornycroft Sturdy ZE 5-ton flat was new to G. T. Sadler, a fruit and vegetable grower of Crowle, near Worcester. It remained in use until 1962, thereafter standing in a field for the next 17 years. When it was purchased by the present owner a condition of the sale was that it was restored to its original livery.

The Thornycroft Sturdy ZE was first introduced in late 1935 and a 3-ton military truck based on the ZE was produced during World War 2.

The vehicle illustrated is powered by a Thornycroft TR6 4.042 litre six-cylinder diesel engine producing 67bhp at 2,200rpm. The final ZE model left the works in April 1950.

Left:
Now owned by Mr F. R. Rankin, of Southport, Lancashire, little is known about the history of this 1950 Commer Superpoise 4-ton tipper other than it was restored by its present owner in 1985/86 after having spent the previous eight years in a field.

The Superpoise was so called because the design featured the front axle in the optimum position for legal weight distribution in a similar fashion to the contemporary Morris-Commercial Equi-load.

Powered by either a 4 litre six-cylinder petrol engine or a Perkins P6 diesel, this version of the Superpoise was available from 1948 until 1955, but preserved examples are not common.

Below:
This illustrates two splendid Sentinel diesel lorries owned and restored by the husband and wife team of Neil and Maggie Matlock, of Sileby, Leicestershire.

On the left is a 1950 DV4/4 8-ton flat which was new to William Tatton (Dyers) of Leek, Staffordshire, its only commercial owner. It was purchased for preservation in 1976, taking an estimated 5,200hr to restore over the next five years! On the right is a 1955 DV4/6T 12-ton tipper which was new to Caldwells of Coventry and used for coal distribution, later being used by a sugar beet farmer near Peterborough, from whom it was rescued in 1981. This lorry took 8½ years to restore.

Both vehicles are powered by the Sentinel-Ricardo 6-litre four-cylinder indirect-injection diesel engine mounted horizontally under the vehicle chassis in similar fashion to the Sentinel S type steamer of the 1930s.

The DV four-wheeler was introduced in 1946, the six-wheeler following in 1948 and both continued in production until 1957, although a limited number of lorries using Sentinel parts were assembled by Transport Vehicles (Warrington) Ltd and know as TVWs.

These three award-winning vehicles belong to the fleet of historic trucks owned by Knowles Transport Ltd, of Wimblington, Cambridgeshire. All are equipped with dropside bodywork. From the left are a 1950 Foden FE6/12 12-tonner, a 1959 ERF 56GTS 10-tonner and a 1953 Foden FE4/8 8-tonner.

The Foden FE6/12 is a heavy duty double-drive six-wheeler, one of a batch of six delivered new to the Ministry of Defence for drawbar use. Featuring the stylish S18 cab, this example is fitted with Foden's own 12-speed gearbox and 8.377 litre six-cylinder two-stroke diesel engine, the sound of which is guaranteed to set a truck enthusiast's pulse racing!

Equally stylish is the KV, or Kleer-Vue, cab fitted to the ERF. This is a Gardner 5LW-powered twin-steer six-wheeler. This wheel arrangement gave the operator a ton or two extra payload over the contemporary two-axle model and this example was new to Humphries of Watford, but was eventually rescued from a farmer's field near Bury St Edmunds and restored by its present owner in 1988.

The Foden FE4/8 is a lightweight four-wheeler fitted with an FD4 2.72 litre four-cylinder version of the two-stroke and a modern-looking cab by Bowyers of Congleton. It was used by the makers until their take-over by Paccar in 1980 and then passed to Barretts Transport before being acquired by Knowles and restored, making its first appearance on the 1991 London-Brighton Run.

This 1951 Guy Otter 6-ton flat is now owned by Mr G. Davis, of Glastonbury, Somerset. Supplied new by Rhodgate Service Station, Cleeve, Bristol, to British Road Services, it was later used by Western Transport, then various other owners before going to J. C. Thomas & Sons Ltd, of Glastonbury, in whose livery it has been restored over a five-year period, after been found on a farm at Chewton Mendip, Somerset. Photographed on the Somerset Levels, this lorry is powered by a Gardner 4LK 3.8 litre diesel, but a 3.7 litre petrol engine was also offered. The Otter was introduced in 1948; a Perkins P6-powered tractor unit was added in 1952, and later models had the Motor Panels cab fitted, as on contemporary Thornycrofts.

41

This 1951 Leyland Beaver 12B 7½-ton flat, now owned by Helsby & Longden Ltd of Frodsham, Cheshire, was originally a National Health Service mobile X-ray van. A number of this type have survived into preservation, often to be restored in road haulage form. This lorry was found in a scrapyard in 1972 and restored to the 1950s livery of its present owners. An example of an historic lorry preserved in working condition, complete with authentically-sheeted load, eagle-eyed readers will spot a present-day intrusion in the form of a CB aerial!

Introduced in 1947 and powered by a Leyland O.600 9.8 litre diesel, the 12B Beaver was a heavy-duty four-wheeler often used with a drawbar trailer. It continued in production until 1954 and has become very much a postwar classic.

This 1952 Atkinson L744 7-ton flat is now owned by Mr V. Evans, of Maes-y-Cwmmer, Mid-Glamorgan. It was new to Chivers Jams at Histon, Cambridgeshire, later passing to showmen in Southampton. It was purchased in derelict condition by the present owner in 1989 and restored. It attended its first rally at Cyforthfa Castle, Merthyr Tydfil, as part of the 150th anniversary celebrations for the Taff Vale Railway.

The Atkinson 744 had a 5.5 litre Gardner 4LW diesel engine and was introduced in 1935, being very much an assembly of proprietary components. As such it was similar to the contemporary ERF. Atkinson Lorries (1933) Ltd had been specifically formed to manufacture diesel lorries, the previous Atkinson company being well-known for manufacturing steam waggons. The Atkinson 'Big A' radiator motif was to become a familiar sight on British roads and by popular demand is still with us today.

Owned by Mr C. Pitt, of Otley, West Yorkshire, this 1952 Vulcan 6PF 6-ton flat was used originally in Essex for the delivery of potatoes and, later, milk. It was restored during 1993/94 to join the well-known Colin Pitt historic commercial vehicle fleet.

The Vulcan 6PF with 4.73 litre Perkins P6 diesel and the 6VF — its petrol-engined equivalent — were introduced in 1939 and built at the Tilling-Stevens factory at Maidstone, Kent. Production of Vulcan had been transferred to Maidstone from the company's old factory at Southport following the Tilling-Stevens take-over in 1936. During World War 2 production was on a very limited basis to austerity standards, with a mesh grille and no brightwork. However, after the war, the Vulcan became quite popular, most notably with British Road Services in tank, tipper and tractor unit form.

Production of Vulcan continued until 1953 after which the name disappeared, following the take-over of Tilling-Stevens by the Rootes Group.

First owned by J. Linham & Sons, Westhay, Meare, Somerset, and used until 1968 for hauling concrete blocks, this 1954 Leyland Comet 90 7$\frac{1}{2}$-ton dropside lorry is now owned by Massey Wilcox Ltd, Chilcompton, Somerset. It was the advent of the annual MoT test that caused a number of older lorries, like this, to be withdrawn at that time. It was discovered in 1991 by the present owners and restored over 2$\frac{1}{2}$ years to represent a similar vehicle operated by the company in the mid-1950s.

The stylish Comet 90, which shared the same Briggs Motor Bodies cab as the Ford Thames and the Dodge Kew, was introduced in 1951 and was powered by the 5.76 litre O.351 diesel engine. It was probably best known in service with Blue Circle Cement, readers of a certain age no doubt being familiar with the Dinky model of this vehicle. The Comet 90 remained in production in truck, tipper and tractor unit form until 1960.

Two well-known goods vehicle types from the 1950s are featured here in the form of a 1955 Dennis Pax 5-tonner and a 1956 Ford Thames 506E 2-tonner, both of which are owned by Mr T. Bailey, of Melksham, Wiltshire.

The Dennis Pax, powered by a Perkins P6 diesel, was new to E. T. Waters, of Manor Farm, Orcheston, Shrewton, which nestles on the southern edge of Salisbury Plain. It was used for hay and straw deliveries, and thus features a prominent Luton extension over the cab to increase its payload capacity. In 1962 the vehicle was retired to a farm outbuilding, where it languished for the next 25 years until being restored over a three-year period to its original condition.

The Ford Thames has a 3.6 litre 4D four-cylinder diesel engine and originally worked as a garage breakdown vehicle in Weston-super-Mare. It was, however, restored as a dropside lorry in 1986.

This 1958 Albion Chieftain FT37KCL 5½-ton flat is owned by Mr
P. Sykes, of Pool-in-Wharfedale, West Yorkshire. A fine example of a
former British Road Services lorry, it spent all its working life at
Stoke-on-Trent depot and was bought for preservation in original
condition in 1986, the only new parts required being two windscreen
glasses and the rear wings.

The Chieftain FT37 was one of Albion's best-known postwar
models and when introduced in 1948 was powered by its 4.88 litre
four-cylinder diesel. Albion was still using the term 'oil' engine for its
diesels in the 1950s and even when this vehicle, one of the last FT37s
built, with the larger 5.5 litre EN.335 engine introduced in 1957, the
'Albion Oil Engine' badge was still being fitted to the radiator.

47

Owned by Mr R. Mothersele of Beaminster, Dorset, this 1959 Albion Chieftain CH3A 7-ton dropside lorry was delivered new to Fowler Bros, animal feed manufacturers of South Chard, Somerset. It was purchased from them by the present owner after being laid up for 23 years.

Introduced in 1958 as a replacement for the old FT37 model, the CH3A had the EN.335 four-cylinder 5.5 litre diesel engine and the Motor Panels 'Vista View' LAD cab that was also fitted to contemporary Leyland and Dodge trucks, Leyland having acquired Albion in 1951.

Some early examples of the CH3A had Holmalloy light-alloy cabs, particularly those in service with British Road Services and the model continued in production until the mid-1960s.

The Chieftain name continued with the CH13 Leyland-powered six-cylinder range until production of Albion-badged vehicles ceased in September 1972, although the name lived on with the Leyland-badged G-cab range produced at the Albion works until 1980.

This 1962 Ford Thames Trader 3-ton dropside lorry is now owned by Mr C. Stone of Bristol. New to Terry & Son, joiners of Clevedon, Somerset, for delivering door and window frames, it only operated locally, thus covering only a very low mileage. When the company ceased trading in 1986 it passed to the present owner and has been restored to original condition featuring factory-fitted bodywork and is finished in the Ford delivery colour of 'Cargo Grey'.

This lorry is a little unusual in that it is powered by a 3.2 litre four-cylinder petrol engine, most of the lighter examples having the 3.6 litre 4D diesel engine.

The Thames Trader was introduced in 1957 and was available from 30cwt up to 7-ton capacity. Up to 3 tons, the four-cylinder petrol or diesel engines were fitted and above that weight had either a 4.8 litre six-cylinder petrol or a 5.4 litre six-cylinder diesel engine.

The type was particularly popular as tippers, including a six-wheel version produced in conjunction with County Commercial Cars. The Thames Trader remained in production until 1965.

Owned by Mr D. Bennie, of Bothwell, Strathclyde, this 1964 ERF LKG44 6½-ton flat is an example of a model popular with the brewing industry as a delivery dray. CSC 235B was new to Scottish Breweries Ltd. A number of the company's former drays have survived into preservation as they were withdrawn with plenty of life left in them as a result of union pressure to adopt three-man crews, which the ERFs could not accommodate. Noted for their low operating costs, mainly due to the economy of the little Gardner 4LK engine, the LKG44 used a smaller version of the KV cab, known as the LKV, and did not have the extra brightwork above and below the distinctive oval grille.

The smallest model in the ERF range, the LKG44 was introduced in 1955 and continued in production until 1964, being the last in the line of Gardner 4LK-engined lightweights which went back to the original OE4 model of 1935.

This 1951 AEC Mammoth Major 6 MkIII 12-ton flat is now owned by Mr R. C. Cresswell, of Hilderstone, Staffordshire. It is a heavy duty double drive six-wheeler that was new to the Air Ministry as a fuel bowser and was later used by a civil engineering company. As these vehicles were non-standard they were eventually built at the Maudslay works in Coventry, which had been taken over by AEC in 1948. It was purchased by the present owner in 1976 and restored as a flat, as seen here carrying a preserved Fordson Model N agricultural tractor.

Powered by the maker's 9.6 litre six-cylinder diesel, the Mammoth Major MkIII was introduced in 1949 and is another classic postwar British truck from the golden era of AEC, which was a leading producer of heavy-duty six-wheelers in the 1950s. Often seen with a drawbar trailer or 'dangler', they were also popular as tankers and tippers, in the latter form particularly with Wimpey.

From about 1954 the MkIII range was fitted with an updated 'tin front' cab which concealed the radiator and was superseded by the MkV range in 1958, although continued to be built until 1960.

Owned by Mr M. Bexton, of Ravenstone, Leicestershire, this 1953 Atkinson L1266 12-ton flat was one of a large number of Atkinsons operated by Bexton & Smith of Coalville, Leicestershire. This lorry has been restored to original condition and really captures the look of a 1950s 'heavy' with its attractive livery and nicely-sheeted load.

The 1266 model Atkinson six-wheeler was first introduced in 1935, but was only produced in very small numbers prior to World War 2. However, the Ministry of Supply placed an order for 60 in 1940 and a further 100 in 1941 for civilian users, the latter being powered by AEC 7.7 litre diesels due to all Gardner 6LW engines being required for military use. After the war, due to continuing shortages in supply, Atkinson designed and built its own five-speed gearbox in 1946 and later that year moved to larger premises at Walton-le-Dale, near Preston. Production continued into the 1950s, with the traditional Atkinson appearance changing very little, but the increase in permitted weight following amendment to the Construction & Use Regulations in 1955 allowed 20-ton gross six-wheelers with a payload of about 13 tons, so the L1266 then became the L1366; only the short wheelbase S1266 continued in production until 1959.

Two Maudslay lorries are seen here in the form of a 1949 Meritor 15-ton dropside eight-wheeler on the left and, also from 1949, a Mogul 7-ton four-wheeled flat on the right. Both are now owned by Mr A. G. Lloyd, of Ludlow, Shropshire.

The Maudslay Meritor was introduced in 1948 and powered by an AEC 9.6 litre diesel, AEC having taken over Maudslay, of Parkside Works, Coventry, during that year to form the Associated Commercial Vehicles group along with Crossley Motors of Stockport.

British Road Services was the main user of the Meritor. Particularly impressive were the boxvans used by BRS Parcels, which featured a substantial front bumper at loading bank height to prevent damage to the massive cast aluminium radiator. The Meritor was produced up until early 1951, by which time 256 had been built.

The Mogul four-wheeler was also AEC-powered, this time by the 7.7 litre diesel, although some had been built with the Gardner 5LW engine. The first Moguls had been built as far back as 1933, but following the AEC take-over the Maudslay models were phased out in favour of the AEC Monarch and Mammoth Major by 1951 and Maudslays after this date were just badge-engineered AECs.

This 1949 Leyland Octopus 22.0/1 15-ton dropside lorry is owned by Mr L. Neild, of Blackley, Manchester. The rigid eight-wheeler was the mainstay of haulage fleets in Great Britain from the end of World War 2 until the mid-1960s, and the Leyland Octopus in service with British Road Services was one of the best-known examples. The vehicle illustrated is a genuine ex-BRS lorry, working in London for 10 years before being transferred to Sheffield. It was disposed of to a showman in 1962 from whom it was purchased derelict by the present owner in 1981. It has been restored to the BRS livery of the 1956-62 period.

This model of Octopus was powered by the 9.8 litre Leyland O.600 six-cylinder diesel, and it had a five-speed gearbox and servo-assisted hydraulic brakes on three of the four axles. It was introduced in 1947 — the Octopus name first being used on rigid eights in 1933 — and continued in production until 1954, when the 24-ton 24.0/4 model succeeded it.

Now owned by Mr L. Janes, of Dagenham, Essex, this 1950 AEC Mammoth Major MkIII 15-ton flat was new to British Road Services at Yalding, Kent, carrying fleet number 2A302. It was later transferred to nearby Marden as fleet number 61F302 and used mainly on ICI work. It was sold by BRS in July 1955, later serving with Elliotts of Bournemouth, before being withdrawn. Purchased by the present owner, it is pictured here on one of its first outings after having been completely restored to original BRS condition with the South Eastern

Division royal blue crest of the 1948-51 period on the cab door.

The MkIII Mammoth Major was another popular eight-wheeler from the late 1940s and through the 1950s. It was renowned for its good air-assisted brakes operating on the front, third and fourth axles. It was normally powered by the well-tried 9.6 litre six-cylinder diesel, but after 1949 the larger 11.3 litre engine was sometimes specified, particularly for drawbar use and at 150bhp made this one of the most powerful eight-wheelers of its day.

Completing a trio of ex-British Road Service eight-wheelers is this 1953 Thornycroft Trusty 15-ton flat owned and restored by Mr R. Neild, of Blackley, Manchester. One of six supplied new to BRS Stratford Group and later working from Southampton and Salisbury, it was originally powered by the maker's NR6 7.88 litre 100bhp diesel, being designated the Trusty PF/NR6. However, this engine was replaced in 1959 by the more powerful 9.83 litre 130bhp QR6 engine introduced in 1955 for the uprated 17-ton Trusty PK/QR6. This lorry was sold at auction in 1962 to Rush Green Motors, near Hitchin, Hertfordshire, and remained there for the next 26 years, until

purchased in July 1988 by the present owner and restored over the following six years. Work included the fitting of a replacement cab and body.

The PF/NR6 was the first Thornycroft road haulage eight-wheeler and was introduced in 1946, although it had been designed and almost reached production stage prior to the outbreak of World War 2. It was significant in that it had air brakes on all four axles, whereas most eight-wheelers of the period were braked on the first, third and fourth axles.

Right:
Simulating a transport cafe breakfast stop are (left) a 1958 Leyland Octopus 24.0/4 17-ton flat owned by Mr M. Wainwright of Preston, Lancashire, and (right) a 1954 Leyland Steer 15.S/1 10-ton brewery dray owned by Mr M. Pyatt, of Cheadle, Staffordshire.

The Octopus was new to Midlands Tar Distillers as a tanker and after 10 years' service was sold to John Hammond Haulage, of Oldbury, who converted it to a flat. Around 1977 the chassis was shortened for conversion to a recovery vehicle, but it was only used in this role for two years before being abandoned. It was purchased by the present owner in 1992 and fully restored to its original length as a flat.

The Leyland Steer was delivered new to Hancocks Brewery, of Cardiff, and was specified with the new '600' series steel cab, as on the 24.0/4 Octopus but on the old series chassis. It was saved from scrap in 1989 and restored to its original condition.

The Octopus eight-wheeler was a familiar vehicle in the 1950s, but the Steer, based on the Beaver four-wheeler, was a twin-steered six-wheeler knows as a 'Chinese six', a wheel arrangement first used in the 1930s by ERF, which gave a 30% increase in payload over the four-wheeler without greatly increasing the unladen weight. Used in conjunction with a trailer, a 'Chinese six' could carry a payload of 17 tons. Both the Octopus and the Steer were powered by the Leyland O.600 9.8 litre diesel.

Right:
This 1959 Foden FG6/24 17-ton flat is now owned by Mr G. Baker, of Weston-super-Mare. A fine example of a Foden maximum weight eight-wheeler, it was new to M. Elliott & Son, of Poole, Dorset, who were well-known Foden users. It was used on general haulage until retired in 1972. It was found in scrap state and restored to its original condition by the present owner.

Equipped with the stylish S20 cab, introduced in 1956, this lorry is powered by the 10.45 litre Gardner 6LX six-cylinder diesel, which was introduced in 1958 in response to the demand for more power for the 24-ton gross eight-wheelers permitted from 1955 onwards.

The Foden FG6 range was first introduced in 1948 with the equally stylish S18 cab and Foden's own two-stroke diesel available as well as the Gardner. In 1958 the startling new S21 cab was introduced for the FG range. This was known as the 'Sputnik' or 'Mickey Mouse' and created quite a stir at the time with its streamlined and rounded appearance.

Owned by Mr E. Wheelwright, of Sowerby Bridge, West Yorkshire, this 1953 Scammell Scarab 3-ton articulated lorry was delivered new to British Railways and operated from their Dewsbury, Yorkshire, depot. It has been restored to original condition. Once such a familiar sight all over the country, these little vehicles were introduced in 1948 in both 3-ton and 6-ton forms, succeeding the original Mechanical Horse first introduced in 1933. They were powered by Scammell's own four-cylinder 2.09 litre side-valve petrol engine, which was mounted with the gearbox in the chassis frame behind the cab. The radiator was mounted in the rear wall of the cab and the air intake was located on the offside of the cab behind the driver's door. Designed for use in congested urban areas, they were equipped with Scammell's own design of automatic coupling gear which speeded up dropping and picking up the trailer. Some 13,000 Scarabs were built with British Railways alone taking 7,500 and the 3-ton version was produced until 1965, the 6-ton continuing until 1967. Diesel versions were introduced in 1952 with the Perkins P4 3.14 litre engine in the 6-tonner, later replaced by the updated 4.203 3.33 litre engine and from 1959 the Perkins 4.99 1.62 litre diesel in the 3-tonner.

This 1962 Bristol HA6G 24-ton gross articulated lorry is owned by Mr D. Tarbuck, of Cannock, Staffordshire. New to British Road Services at Oldbury in October 1962 with fleet number 1E1092, it worked between the Midlands and South Wales until 1970, then on local work for two years before being withdrawn. The unit has not been restored but is preserved in the working condition it was in when retired. It is coupled to a York 26ft semi-trailer, which was new to BRS Newport also in 1962.

Developed specifically for BRS, the Bristol HA tractor units were introduced in 1955 together with the ST-type semi-trailer and were claimed as the first articulated vehicles to take advantage of the new Construction & Use Regulations permitting a 24-ton gross weight on four axles. Early examples were designated HA6L and were powered by the 9.8 litre Leyland O.600 engine, but from 1960 the 10.45 litre Gardner 6LX engine was specified in the HA6G (as illustrated) and the 11.1 litre Leyland O.680 in the HA6LL. The final type of GRP cab fitted to the HA is illustrated and in this form it continued in production until April 1964, a total of 653 of all versions being built.

This 1966 AEC Mandator Mk V tractor unit is slightly unusual in that it was originally destined for export and came out of the company's Southall works in CKD (completely knocked down) form. It was assembled by Arlington Motors in Bristol and sold to the Distillers Co Ltd for use on the United Yeast night trunk operation between Bristol and Haydock near Liverpool. This trunk was well known in transport circles and carried on well into the 1980s, when the Bristol factory was closed and subsequently demolished. The Mandator was later downgraded to a wrecker, based at Haydock, but was then purchased by Mr R. Masters of Evesham and restored to period Distillers Co Ltd livery, as seen here.

The AEC Mk V range was announced at the 1958 Commercial Motor Show, the Mandator G4RA tractor unit in the form seen here having an 8ft 1in wheelbase and an AEC AV691 11.3 litre engine developing a creditable 205bhp. With their stylish Park Royal cabs and powerful engine, the Mk V range was successful and popular with over 6,000 of all versions built up to the end of normal production in 1964.

Another interesting comparison shows the advances made from the early postwar years to the late 1960s in the British commercial vehicle industry.

The vehicle on the right is a 1948 Leyland 12.B/1 Beaver from the drawbar era with a Dyson 8-ton trailer giving a 24-ton gross train weight. Originally owned by British Ropes of Retford, it then passed into showman's use, but was purchased for preservation in 1972 and has been restored in Crows of Gateshead livery.

The 1967 Foden 4TXB/30 tractor unit on the left represents the massive shift towards articulation that followed the 1964 Construction & Use Regulations which permitted articulated vehicles to operate at up to 32 tons gross vehicle weight.

Originally owned by Northumberland County Council Parks Division, it has now also been restored in Crows livery and is owned by Mr R. Crow of Ovington, Northumberland.

Whilst the Leyland represents the years of postwar austerity, the Foden was very much a product of 1960s styling, with much use of fibreglass in the distinctive S36 cab.

Right:
Seen in the yard of Bostocks of Congleton, Cheshire, in April 1995 this line up of classic British heavy commercials all dates from more than 20 years ago. It is particularly notable that all three vehicles have been restored by Bostocks for revenue earning service with the company.

The vehicle nearest the camera was built in 1969 as an Atkinson Silver Knight and was new to Warings of Preston for general haulage. It was rebuilt by ex-Atkinson employees in 1978 and plated at the Seddon-Atkinson plant in Oldham.

This vehicle is fitted with a Gardner 6LXB engine, as are the 1974 ERF A-series in the centre, the 1973 Atkinson Raider on the left and the 1973 Atkinson Searcher six-wheeler that the company also possesses but which is not illustrated. This last-mentioned vehicle is now in its seventh year of operation with Bostocks, and is sometimes seen by the authors, at work in the West Country.

Left:
An example of a vehicle that does most of its work off public roads and out of the public eye is this 1940 Unipower Forester Model G timber tractor that was new to Darke & Son, haulage and timber contractor of Hyton Road, Worcester. It was used by them until 1956 when it was sold to C. H. Lambe & Sons of Bromsgrove. Since August 1990 it has been owned by Mr S. Elliott. The photograph was taken with the assistance of the organisers of the Down Rally near Petersfield in Hampshire on 1 July 1995.

Unipower vehicles were first built in 1938 by Universal Power Drives of Perivale, Middlesex, and the Forester was one of the company's best known models, remaining in production with continual improvement for almost 30 years. The present day Unipower Vehicles Ltd manufactures specialist vehicles for military and emergency use, some models having been previously produced by Scammell.

One of the most durable commercial vehicles ever produced in the UK must be the famous AEC O853 Matador, originally introduced in 1939 as a Medium Artillery Tractor for the British Army. After the war many surplus vehicles were sold off for civilian use with a number still in service today. The example illustrated, dating from 1941, was purchased by the Bristol Tramways & Carriage Co Ltd (from 1957 the Bristol Omnibus Co) and, as was often the case, rebodied. In this case panels recognisable as those fitted to contemporary Bristol single-deck buses by Eastern Coachworks of Lowestoft have been used. The vehicle was based at Gloucester Garage and was photographed at St John the Baptist church, Huntley, Gloucestershire. An example of the AEC Matador in original military form can be seen on page 75.

Left:
This 1931 Crossley Condor breakdown tender is now owned by City of Portsmouth Transport Museum. Originally double-deck bus No 74, with a Short 48-seat rear-entrance body, in the Portsmouth fleet, it was converted to its present form in 1948 and as such is the only Crossley Condor known to survive. Introduced in 1930 the Condor was produced by Crossley Motors, of Gorton, Manchester, and this example featured the company's own 9.12 litre direct-injection diesel engine. This made Crossley the first manufacturer in Britain to offer a diesel-engined double-deck bus.

The Condor continued in production until 1936 and the Portsmouth vehicles survived well into the postwar years. At that time it was quite normal practice for bus operators to convert withdrawn vehicles into breakdown tenders and several examples of these have survived into preservation. Thanks are due to Mr Cliff Burgess of the City of Portsmouth Transport Museum for his assistance in obtaining this photograph.

Right:
This 1958 Morris FFK 140 recovery vehicle was new to Wadham Stringer at Waterlooville, Hampshire, and later was based at the company's Melksham depot. It is still an operational vehicle, based at Dilton Marsh Garage, Westbury, Wiltshire, where it has been restored by owner Mr Alan Large.

The FFK was produced by both Austin and Morris between 1958 and 1966 with minor variations to the front grille and was available in 5- or 7-ton models, the 7-tonner being the heaviest rigid vehicle the two companies produced at that time. Austin and Morris had merged in 1952 to create the British Motor Corporation (BMC). The type was also available as a tractor unit. The range was powered by either a 5.1 or a 5.7 litre BMC diesel; the lighter rigids also had the option of a 4 litre petrol engine.

Here are two examples of the specialist conversions available on the well known Thames Trader (see also page 49). Both vehicles have been converted to all-wheel drive drilling rigs and were photographed together at the HCVS South West Area Yeovilton Rally in September 1993.

On the left is a 1965 6x6 formerly used by the London Brick Co and now owned by Mr and Mrs Marshallsays of Wareham, Dorset. Whilst on the right is a 1960 4x4 example that was formerly owned by the Department of Transport Materials Testing Laboratory at South Ruislip and is now owned by Mr P. Spacklen, also of Wareham.

These conversions were carried out by All Wheel Drive Ltd of Camberley. This company also produced factory approved double-drive six-wheeled goods vehicle conversions with both single and double-drive models also available from Ford in conjunction with County Commercial Cars of Fleet, Hampshire.

Photographed at the end of the 1995 HCVS Pendle Run from Leyland to Keighley, this finely restored 1956 Scammell Mountaineer heavy haulage ballast tractor was new to Monks, civil engineers of Warrington, later passing to Martindale of Chorley.

Its last working role was plant hauling on the Keilder Dam project in Northumberland during the early 1980s, but in 1983 it was bought by its present owner, Mr D. Smith of Eastburn, near Keighley. The vehicle is unusual in that it was one of only two built with a crew cab. However, an interesting fact about the standard cab for such a large

vehicle was that it was the same as fitted to the O-type Bedford and Scammell Scarab 'mechanical horse', both tiny vehicles by comparison.

Despite its size, the Mountaineer was the smallest of the Scammell family of heavy haulage lorries introduced in the late 1940s, being in effect a 4x4 version of the 6x6 Constructor, and it was also popular for use as a dump truck. The example illustrated is powered by an 8.4 litre Gardner 6LW diesel, although Meadows and Rolls-Royce engines were also available as an option.

An interesting comparison between production models of British and Swedish commercial vehicles in the late 1960s. The AEC, on the right, is a 1968 TG4R Mandator which, following the 1962 merger between Associated Commercial Vehicles and Leyland, carries the Ergomatic cab first seen at the 1964 Commercial Motor Show and subsequently fitted to AEC, Albion and Leyland models. The vehicle was new to Theodore Emms of Cox's Lane, Netherton, but was only used for two years when, following an industrial dispute, it was parked out of use

from 1970 until 1989. It was then acquired by its present owner, Mr R. Hingley of Brierley Hill, and restored over a three-year period.

The Scania Vabis LB76 illustrated was the first right-hand drive example imported from Sweden in 1966 and was used by B&W Motors of Wolverhampton as a demonstrator for two years before being sold to haulier J. Round of Dudley, from whom it was also purchased in 1982 by Mr Hingley for preservation.

Many historic commercial vehicles in preservation owe their existence to the fact that they were bought second-hand by showmen for fairground use and thus continued in service long after their expected lives in road haulage would have ended.

This is particularly true of Gardner-engined vehicles and the bonnetted Scammell has long been a favourite type with former heavy haulage ballast-box tractors and articulated units being adapted for fairground work, with flamboyant liveries and promotional names often being applied to each vehicle.

The leading vehicle in the photograph is a 1960 Scammell Highwayman, 'The Equalizer', owned and regularly worked by Mr R. J. Rawlins, Supreme Amusements of Ashford, Middlesex. The vehicle behind is a 1942 Scammell, 'Pride of the South', owned by J. Beach & Sons, also of Ashford. They were photographed on the A303 near Andover *en route* to Salisbury for the Autumn Charter Fair on 19 October 1991.

The bonnetted Scammell Tractors unit can be traced right back to 1920 with the design being steadily developed up until the last example was built in 1969. The name Highwayman was introduced in 1958.

This 1964 AEC 2GM4RA Mercury MkII was originally a Simon Snorkel hydraulic escape platform with Hull Fire Brigade, but was purchased by its present owner, Mr Bob Hatcher of Swindon, in 1989 as a derelict chassis/cab. It was restored over a two-year period to a Beaver tail flat for transporting the 1947 Fordson Major E27N tractor as seen in the photograph.

First introduced in 1953 the AEC Mercury, although designed as a goods vehicle, became quite popular as the basis for a variety of fire appliances, examples of which can be seen in preservation today. The 14-ton gvw MkII version of the Mercury was introduced in 1956 and was powered by the AEC AV470 7.7 litre engine. The model continued in production until the new tilt cab Ergomatic range replaced it in 1965.

Also produced as a tractor unit for a gross train weight of either 18 or 22 tons, the Mercury was extremely popular, particularly with British Road Services and by 1964 nearly 10,000 had been built.

This 1942 Leyland Titan TD7 with Merryweather 100ft turntable ladder was delivered new to the National Fire Service in Lincoln and originally carried wartime grey livery.

Six of these appliances were built for the NFS and were based on the TD7 bus chassis, hence the half-cab driving compartment.

The vehicle was powered by a Leyland 8.6 litre diesel engine, whilst the four-section ladder was driven mechanically by the vehicle engine and could be raised to 100ft in 30sec.

After World War 2 it was repainted red and served with the City of Lincoln Fire Service in whose livery it has been preserved. This impressive appliance is now cared for by the Lincolnshire Road Transport Museum situated at North Hykeham, Lincoln, and is part of the museum's impressive collection of historic vehicles that were once all locally operated.

This 1943 Austin K4 Escape Carrier fire appliance was new to the Pembroke Dock Fire Service. It carries bodywork built to the wartime Home Office specification for National Fire Service vehicles. It passed into the Dock's reserve fleet, based at Milford Haven, in 1973 and was then stored in the open, outside a small wooden-built museum for 10 years. It then came to Mr E. Pitcher of Odiham for restoration. This was completed in 1986, apart from the Bayley ladder, which was restored the following winter.

Austin had re-entered the larger commercial vehicle market in 1939, after a gap of some 20 years, with its K-series range, also popularly referred to as the 'Birmingham Bedford' due to a certain similarity in appearance to the contemporary O-type Bedford. These Austins were widely used by the military as ambulances, GS trucks and even airfield crash tenders. The civilian chassis were widely used for a variety of fire appliance purposes, for, in addition to the Escape Carrier on the 5-ton K4, the smaller 2-3 ton K2 was the standard Auxiliary Towing Vehicle with the National Fire Service, used for towing the ubiquitous trailer pumps ordered by the Home Office.

The power unit for the wartime K-series was Austin's own robust 3.5 litre six-cylinder petrol engine.

Representing a classic fire engine of the 1950s, this 1954 Dennis F8 water tender with Dennis bodywork and 500gal/min water pump was new to Derbyshire Fire Service and was originally based at Somercoates. It moved to the then new fire station at Alfreton in about 1960. It was sold in 1977 and stripped of all fittings. Bought by its present owner, Mr Brett Clayton of Middleton Tyas, Darlington, who is a serving fireman, in 1979, it has been restored over a three-year period. In 1983 it was the outright winner of the first HCVS Tyne-Tees Run and readers may recognise the vehicle as the fire engine used in the 'Heartbeat' television series.

Introduced in 1952, the Dennis F8 was powered by a Rolls-Royce B60 4.25 litre six-cylinder petrol engine and continued in production until 1960.

Fitted with bodywork manufactured by James Whiston, this 1950 Commer QX limousine water tender was new to Wiltshire Fire Brigade and stationed at Amesbury and Salisbury before ending its service days as a driver trainer unit. It was sold at auction and restored by Mike and Ian Widgery of Cullompton, Devon, in 1981 to fully operational condition.

This Commer represents a fine example of an early postwar fire appliance where standard forward-control vehicle chassis were utilised to give added storage space with a fully-enclosed crew compartment as standard. The water tender appliance was favoured by more rural and outlying area brigades as they were more capable of carrying some 400gal of water to incidents where water supplies were often inadequate. Commer and Bedford chassis were particularly favoured.

The Commer QX was introduced in 1948 and rated as a 5-tonner. It was originally powered by the Commer 4.57 litre six-cylinder petrol engine, which was held in very high regard by the transport industry at that time, although later versions had the Rootes TS3 two-stroke diesel or the Perkins 6.354 diesel.

A number of similar appliances have survived into preservation and Commer continued to be a popular choice for fire appliances until the name was dropped in 1976 in favour of Dodge.

This 1942 Chevrolet C15A 15cwt 4x4 GS truck is owned by Mr D. Austin of Frome, Somerset, and is a fine example of a Canadian Military Pattern (CMP) vehicle produced in very large numbers by both Chevrolet and Ford in Ontario, Canada, during World War 2. The two companies had agreed to merge their resources for military production in 1936 and the first CMP vehicles came to Britain with the Canadian forces in December 1939. The range consisted of vehicles from 8cwt up to 3-ton as well as utilities, ambulances and field artillery tractors. The two makes were outwardly almost identical, although the most obvious difference was the diagonal mesh grille, as illustrated, on the Chevrolet as opposed to the square mesh pattern on the Ford. Mechanically there were a number of differences; the Chevrolet had a straight six 'Stovebolt Six' engine and the Ford the familiar V8 unit.

The cab type seen here was introduced in 1942 as the No 13, replacing earlier designs which were criticised for the cramped driving position.

The total output of military motor vehicles from Canada in World War 2 was over 815,000. Production was particularly significant for the amount of standardisation and the integration of British design features, like forward control and large single tyres, with American engineering (engines, transmission and axles) and mass production techniques.

The vehicle shown carries the markings of the 8th Army 13th Corps as used during the North Africa campaign.

After the war many of these vehicles were purchased for civilian use, particularly as recovery vehicles, logging tractors etc, and some are still operational today — a testimony to the sound, rugged design.

A fine pair of AEC Matadors photographed at the HCVS East Anglia Area's West Bergholt Rally in July 1994, featuring on the left a 1942 Medium Artillery Tractor and on the right a 1944 ex-RAF flat. These are now owned by Mr P. Smith and Mr R. Reed respectively, both of North Chingford, Essex. Introduced in 1939, the AEC Matador O853 was developed from an FWD/Hardy design of the early 1930s and was powered by the well known AEC 7.7 litre diesel engine. A total of 8,612 Medium Artillery Tractors were built and were used to haul such pieces as the 3.7in anti-aircraft gun at home and the 5.5in howitzer in the field. The RAF version was much less common, the 400 built being mainly fitted with flat platform bodywork. After the war Matadors became a familiar sight in civilian use as recovery vehicles, timber tractors and fairground tractors for example and a number are still at work today (see page 63).

Another fine pair of ex-military vehicles at the same event were these two Scammell SV/2S recovery vehicles. The vehicle on the left is a 1944 model in army livery now owned by Mr J. Cardwell of Little Bromley and that on the right is a 1945 example in RAF livery owned by Mr N. Everett of Dedham.

Officially classified as Heavy Breakdown Tractors, these vehicles shared much in common with the Scammell Pioneer R100 Heavy Artillery Tractor and the Tank Transporter Tractor, all being fitted with the Gardner 6LW engine and six-speed gearboxes, although the Tank Transport Tractor had a slightly longer wheelbase at 15ft compared to the other versions which were 12ft 2in.

The origin of these durable vehicles can be traced back to the original Scammell Pioneer 6x4 truck of 1927 with its transversely sprung front axle and rear axle bogies consisting of rocking balancer beam containing gear cases with a driven wheel at each outer end.

The SV/2S was introduced in 1939 and some 1,500 were built up to 1946. Just like the AEC Matador, many of these vehicles passed into civilian use after World War 2 and a number are still operational today.

Photographed on a raw April day, this 1952 Scammell Explorer 6x6 Recovery Tractor with Meadows 6PC630 10.35 litre six-cylinder petrol engine was new to the Royal Electrical & Mechanical Engineers (REME), whose insignia can be seen on the radiator guard.

Developed from the wartime Scammell SV/2S, these impressive looking vehicles were introduced in 1950 and the first 125 comprised Scammell's first postwar military vehicle contract. Exported to the armies of Egypt and New Zealand, the type was also used by the RAF as a heavy drawbar tractor with a ballast box body.

The specification featured a six-speed gearbox with overdrive top and two-speed transfer, air brakes and a 15-ton winch.

Another well known military vehicle from the early postwar years was the Humber 1-ton 4x4 and this 1953 wireless truck is now owned by Mr M. Gumbrill of Stevenage. Although photographed at West Bergholt Rally, apart from the civilian registration number, this fully-equipped vehicle could almost be somewhere on manoeuvres with the British Army.

Introduced in 1952, this type of vehicle superseded the old wartime 15cwt designs (mainly Bedfords and Morris-Commercial) as a high mobility combat truck. They were produced by Rootes at the old Tilling-Stevens factory at Maidstone but used the Humber name to continue the association with such vehicles begun in World War 2 with the Humber FWD.

Powered by the Rolls-Royce B60 4.25 litre six-cylinder petrol engine and with a top speed of 55mph, these vehicles were used for a variety of roles from GS truck to armoured truck (the Humber Pig), examples of which are still in operational military use today.

Below:

A fitting photograph with which to end this volume of historic commercial vehicles, I hope you will agree!

The vehicle featured is a lovely old-timer in the form of a 1924 Leyland A1 2-ton flat owned by Mr R. Harris of Gillingham, Dorset. Mr Graham Hacker is playing the role of a lorry driver of a bygone era, snatching a few hours of well-earned rest slumped over the steering wheel after a long and arduous day on the road at a legal 12mph.

Life was not easy for the 1920s lorry driver, for nearly everything was 'handballed' and had to be roped and sheeted (no curtainsiders in those days!) and the engine started by swinging the handle with a hand throttle lever on the steering wheel to assist.

Speeds were very slow and the roads very poor by today's standards, but lorries like this and the vast number of ex-WD vehicles left over from World War 1 stimulated the growth of the road haulage industry in a massive way.

Front cover:

This 1951 Bedford KD 30cwt with hand-operated tipping gear was new to a haulage contractor in Weston-super-Mare. It subsequently worked for a scrap merchant in Congresbury and then on a farm in Wellington, Somerset, before ending up as a dustcart at a Somerset holiday camp. It was recently refurbished by the present owner, Mr John Smith of Frome, Somerset, and was photographed at Shearwater Lake near Warminster, Wiltshire.

Back cover:

Owned originally by T. Silcock & Sons of Halstall near Ormskirk, Lancashire, this 1948 Seddon Mk5L flat remained in use with its original owners until 1980. It then stood disused until purchased by the present owner, Mr Joe Longson of Preston, in 1985. It was restored over a three-year period to its original condition. We thought an apt title for this photograph would be 'Warehouse Wait', and thanks are due to the owner and Mr Maurice White of the Cheshire Road Run for their assistance.

The 'Heyday' series from IAN ALLAN *Publishing*